PASSPORT MEXICO

2nd Edition

D0644848

Passport to the World

Passport Argentina
Passport Brazil
Passport China
Passport France
Passport Germany
Passport Hong Kong
Passport India
Passport Israel
Passport Italy
Passport Japan
Passport Korea
Passport Malaysia
Passport Mexico
Passport Philippines
Passport Poland
Passport Russia
Passport Singapore
Passport South Africa
Passport Spain
Passport Switzerland
Passport Taiwan
Passport Thailand
Passport United Kingdom
Passport USA
Passport Vietnam

PASSPORT
MEXICO

Your Pocket Guide
to
Mexican Business,
Customs & Etiquette

2nd Edition

Randy Malat

Passport Series Editor: Barbara Szerlip

WORLD TRADE PRESS®
Books and E-Content for International Trade

World Trade Press
1450 Grant Avenue, Suite 204
Novato, California 94945 USA
Tel: (415) 898-1124
Fax: (415) 898-1080
USA Order Line: (800) 833-8586
E-mail: sales@worldtradepress.com
www.worldtradepress.com
www.worldtraderef.com
www.globalroadwarrior.com

Passport Mexico, 2nd Edition
ISBN 1-885073-91-7
"Passport to the World" concept: Edward Hinkelman
Cover design: Peter Jones
Illustrations: Tom Watson

Disclaimer
This publication is designed to provide general information con-
cerning the cultural aspects of doing business with people from a
particular country. It is sold with the understanding that the pub-
lisher is not engaged in rendering legal or any other professional
services. If legal advice or other expert assistance is required, the
services of a competent professional person should be sought.

Library of Congress Cataloging-in-Publication Data
Malat, Randy, 1957–
Passport Mexico: your pocket guide to Mexican business, customs
& etiquette / Randy Malat. -- 2nd ed.
p. cm. -- (Passport to the world)
Includes bibliographic references.
ISBN 1-885073-91-7
1. Business etiquette -- Mexico. 2. Corporate culture -- Mexico.
3. Business communication -- Mexico. 4. Negotiation in business --
Mexico. I. Title. II. Series.
HF5389.3.M6M35 2003
390'.00972 -- dc21

2003041114

Printed in the United States of America

Table of Contents
Mexico

The Moon's Navel

1 Doing Business Across Cultures

Internationally Speaking

Although business operations around the world have become highly standardized, national traditions, attitudes and beliefs remain diverse. Everyone's perceptions — what we see, hear, taste, touch and smell — are filtered through a particular set of habits and assumptions. When you understand that your own cultural background colors your world view, you can begin to appreciate that your foreign associate may have an entirely different perspective, and that he or she may approach a situation in a totally different and unexpected way.

For example, whereas Westerners tend to value individuality of thought and action, Eastern cultures prize conformity and harmony of purpose. While an Englishman's primary focus may be to conclude the matter at hand, people from Latin cultures will concentrate on first developing a personal relationship.

Passport Mexico

Passport Mexico will introduce you to Mexico's business culture and offer insights into how local traditions, etiquette, values and communication styles differ from your own.

Comparing Values Across Cultures

One Culture:	Another Culture:
Values change	Values tradition
Favors specific communication	Favors ambiguous communication
Values analytical, linear problem solving	Values intuitive, lateral problem solving
Places emphasis on individual performance	Places emphasis on group performance
Considers verbal communication most important	Considers context & nonverbal communication most important
Focuses on task and product	Focuses on relationship and process
Places emphasis on promoting differing views	Places emphasis on harmony and consensus
Emphasizes competition	Emphasizes collaboration
Prefers informal tone	Prefers formal tone
Is flexible about schedules	Emphasizes rigid adherence to schedules

Mexico
Quick Look

Official name	Los Estados Unidos Mexicanos
Land area	1,972,550 sq km
Capital & largest city	Mexico City (Distrito Federal)
	Population: 21 million
Elevations	Highest–Volcan Pico de Orizaba 5,700m
	Lowest–Sea level along coasts

People

Population	103,400,165 (2002)
Density	52.41 per sq km
Distribution	75% urban, 25% rural
Annual growth	1.47%
Official language	Spanish
Major religions	Roman Catholic (89%), Protestant (6%)

Economy

GDP	US$920 billion
	US$9,000 per capita
Foreign trade	Imports—US$168 billion
	Exports—US$159 billion
Import partners	US 68.4%; Japan 4.7%
	Germany 3.6%; Canada 2.5%
	China 2.2%; S. Korea 2.1%
Export partners	US 88%; Canada 2%
	Germany 0.9%; Spain 0.8%
Currency	1 peso = 100 centavos

Education and health

Literacy	89%
Hospital beds	0.8 per 1,000 persons
Physicians	1.2 per 1,000 persons
Life expectancy	Women—75.21 years
	Men—68.9 years
Infant mortality	24.52 per 1,000 live births

MEXICO

2   Country Facts

Geography and Demographics

Mexico is the world's 13th largest country, three times the size of Texas and bigger than Spain, France, Germany, Italy, and Great Britain combined. Its border with the United States spans over 3,300 km (2,100 miles). From Tijuana in Mexico's northwest corner to the southern boundary with Guatemala is about the same distance as from London to sub-Saharan Africa. Mexico's 10,000 km (6,000 miles) of coastline front on the Pacific Ocean, the Gulf of Mexico and the Caribbean.

Mexico's population has grown to more than 100 million and half of all Mexicans are under the age of 20. Most people live in urban areas on the broad central plateau. The northern half of the country, though the site of several of the country's biggest cities, is, for the most part, a sparsely populated expanse of grazing lands, farms, mountains and desert. Mexico City is the world's most populous city; nearly one of every four Mexicans lives within its greater metropolitan area. The capital dominates the country's economic, political and cultural life, much as it did prior to the Spanish conquest in 1521.

The Mexican people are predominantly *mestizo*, a legacy of the "encounter" between the Spanish colonists and the Native Americans. Over eight of every ten Mexicans have some mixture of Spanish and indigenous blood; about ten percent of the population is indigenous.

Climate

Mexico's terrain ranges from desert to tropical rainforest and from coastal to mountainous. The north is arid. The tropical southern half features hot, wet coastal plains.

Though Mexico City is at about the same latitude as Hawaii and Bombay, its elevation (2,240 meters, 7,250 feet above sea level) makes for moderate year-round temperatures, ranging from January's 5–21°C (41–70°F) to 10–27°C (50–81°F) in May and October.

Guadalajara, Mexico's second city, is lower (1,590 meters, 5,150 feet) and warmer than the capital. In Monterrey, the largest northern city, temperatures range from freezing nights in December and January to 40°C (104° F) or more on summer days. The same is true of rapidly growing border cities like Ciudad Juárez and Mexicali. Tijuana (adjacent to San Diego) enjoys a warm climate protected from extremes by the ocean and summer fog.

In central and southern Mexico, the dry season lasts from October to mid-June. At this time (especially December through February), Mexico City's legendary smog is at its worst. The heat builds until summer rains clean the air in the big cities and turn the parched countryside green.

November to February are the best months to visit beaches and Mayan ruins in the tropical lowlands, which become hot and humid in spring and are lashed by monsoon-like storms in summer.

Business Hours

Banks open at 9 A.M. and conduct business until 1:30 P.M. with limited transactions between 4 p.m. and 6 p.m. Business office hours are 9 A.M. to 6 P.M., with a two-hour break for lunch (called siesta). Retail stores are generally open from 9 A.M. until 9 P.M., but have shorter hours during winter. Government office hours are 9 A.M. to 1 P.M. All businesses are open Monday through Friday, while retail shops also remain open with limited hours through Saturday and Sunday.

National Holidays

New Year's Day .... January 1
Constitution Day .... February 5
Benito Juárez's Birthday .... March 21
Good Friday and Easter .... Late March/April
Labor Day .... May 1
Cinco de Mayo
(Battle of Puebla Day) .... May 5
President's Annual Message........... September 1
Declaration of Independence Day... September 15
Independence Day........................... September 16
Day of the Race (Columbus Day) ... October 12
All Saints/All Souls Day................... November 1–2
Anniversary of the Mexican
    Revolution .... November 20
Day of Our Lady of Guadalupe .... December 12
Christmas.. December 25

Most businesses, banks and government offices are closed on the holidays listed above. Regional festivals close down businesses for a day or two. Nationwide, business slows to a crawl between Christmas and New Year's and during the week prior to Easter (*semana santa*, or holy week).

3 The Mexicans

Language

Mexico is the most populous Spanish-speaking country in the world. Ninety-eight percent of all Mexicans speak Spanish. About six million have, as their mother tongue, one of over 50 indigenous languages and dialects (another 139 are believed lost); about 1.25 million speak these indigenous tongues exclusively.

Numerous place names and words used in vernacular speech come from Nahuatl (the Aztec language, still spoken in parts of central Mexico) and other indigenous languages. Many foods — such as *elote* (corn), *aguacate* (avocado), *cacahuate* (peanut), and *pozole* (corn and pork soup) — are known by their traditional names. "Mexico" literally means "the moon's navel."

Mexicans delight in their language and treat conversation as an art form. They are adept at rapid verbal exchange, clever word play, joke telling and using colorful sayings. At the same time, the language is highly formalized, characterized by self-consciously polite ways of making requests, asserting opinions and expressing disagreement. While it is not absolutely necessary to know Spanish in order to operate in Mexico, familiarity with the language will endear a visitor to Mexicans and allow a window into the national character.

As of 2002, the official adult literacy rate was 89 percent. But literacy rates are lower in rural areas and in the poorest states (about 75 percent in Guerrero, Oaxaca and Chiapas). Moreover, one out of every three Mexicans over the age of 15 either did not finish or never attended primary school. Steady population growth and a shortage of resources for education will continue to hamper efforts to make all Mexicans functionally literate.

English is widely taught in public and private schools, but with a focus on reading comprehension and written grammar. Most Mexicans who speak English fluently are found among the technocratic, academic and cultural elite, in tourism, or in the U.S. border area. A small number of elites speak French or German as well.

The Family

The family is the most important institution in Mexican society. It commands the individual's full commitment and offers a place where Mexicans can drop their formality and restraint.

For both economic and traditional reasons, children usually live with their parents until they marry, even well into their 30s. If they stay single, they are likely to remain at home for life. In many working class families, a son who marries brings his wife into the family home.

Family members also tend to socialize together. Extended family groups gather on weekends and holidays; dispersed family members take overnight buses to spend time with their kin. There is nothing unusual about three generations vacationing together, perhaps accompanied by aunts, uncles and cousins, along with close family friends.

The family serves as the country's primary social welfare agency; members pool their earnings to make ends meet. They help one another find jobs and count on each other for loans. For most Mexicans, it would be unthinkable to refuse to lend a hand or one's savings to a relative in need.

Family members are likely to work together as well. According to government statistics, nearly 80 percent of the work force is employed in enterprises involving five or fewer employees. Most of these entities are family businesses — ventures ranging from shops, restaurants, and small factories to taco stands and other forms of street vending.

Family events, duties and problems often take precedence over business or other outside matters. Though many Mexicans admire those who single-mindedly strive for achievement outside the home, such people are apt to be seen as selfish, overly ambitious, having confused priorities, and perhaps not to be trusted.

To say Mexicans are family-oriented is not to say that all Mexican families are models of harmonious cooperation. Though divorce rates are low, family desertion is common and many children are born out of wedlock. By some estimates, more than 30 percent or more of Mexico's families are headed by single mothers.

Religion

The Catholic Church is a powerful force in Mexican society. Over 90 percent of the populace is Catholic, though 40 percent or fewer are regular churchgoers. Religious observance is strongest among the lower classes, women, the elderly, and in small towns. The Virgin of Guadalupe is venerated nationwide, and many Mexicans pay homage to saints affiliated with specific localities and occupations.

The vast majority of children are baptized and receive First Communion. Although religious weddings are not legally recognized, most civil marriage proceedings are followed by a church wedding. Some Mexicans regard only the latter as a legitimate union and believe that couples who take vows solely before a judge have not married properly. About seven of every ten adults oppose legalizing abortion, a reflection of the Church's influence on morality.

Many have noted a strong fatalism in the Mexican character: a belief that a mystical, all-powerful force controls the universe, and that one has only limited control over one's fate. This idea dates back to indigenous religions and has been reinforced by Catholic doctrine and the country's long-suffering history.

This sense of powerlessness and resignation is not unrealistic, given implacable socioeconomic barriers that make upward mobility difficult, and the fact that struggle and merit often go unrewarded. The oft-heard phrase *Si Dios quiere* (God willing) expresses this world view.

Dignity and Respect

While most Mexicans are apt to believe their fate is in God's hands, they place special value on carrying themselves with dignity in daily life and on receiving respect from others. They are on guard against *hacer el ridículo* (making fools of themselves) and ever watchful for what they consider disrespectful treatment. This preoccupation with manners and respect stems from both indigenous and Spanish traditions.

From the Mexican perspective, dignity is a measure of one's worth. One maintains it by being polite and respectful to others, being soft-spoken, patient, self-effacing, avoiding emotional outbursts and remaining calm under stress. Dignity is akin to the Asian concept of "face"; staying in control of one's actions reinforces one's status among peers.

Interestingly, Mexicans use the same adjective (*bien educado*) both for "having good manners" and "being well educated." Good manners encompass everything from deferential treatment of elders and employers to not interrupting when others speak; from respecting other's opinions to finding a face-saving way to say "no"; from treating women in a courtly way to dressing and grooming oneself neatly; from picking up the check at a restaurant to going out of one's way to assist others.

In the context of this code, disrespect is likely to be seen as a breach of trust, an insult or even a challenge. A worker who feels mistreated may quit his job, even at the price of economic hardship. An individual who feels he has been slighted in front of family members, friends, or business associates may feel compelled to retaliate somehow.

How the Mexicans View Themselves

Mexicans generally see themselves as a people with strong moral and spiritual values, such as family unity, selflessness and generosity. While they lament being poorer materially than some other nationalities (particularly their northern neighbor), they value their spontaneity, humor, and knack for enjoying life. They take pride in having warm human relationships and in being welcoming to strangers. While they are unlikely to describe themselves in such terms, their behavior demonstrates these qualities.

At the same time, many Mexicans are quick to be critical of their own shortcomings. It is common to hear Mexicans describe their homeland as backward, corrupt or undemocratic, its way of doing things as inefficient and exasperating, and its people as impossible to organize. However, they dislike outsiders pointing out these weaknesses.

Attitudes Toward Other Cultures

Mexico's colonization by Spain and later by France, compounded with its three-time invasion by the United States (to whom it was forced to cede half of its territory) have all fed a general distrust of foreigners.

Mexicans reserve their most conflicting attitudes for their neighbor to the north. They view North Americans as cold, materialistic and overbearing; at the same time, they admire *gringo* democracy, prosperity and technological achievement. The "American way of life" makes ever deeper inroads into Mexican culture by way of mass media, consumer products and ongoing cross-cultural interaction. (Disneyland and Disney World are popular destinations for millions of middle- and upper-class Mexican families.) Still, some Mexicans see "cultural imperialism" in the guise of everything from the new McDonald's franchise in the neighborhood to Hollywood's near-monopoly over Mexican movie screens, from the adoption of revealing dress styles by Mexican youth to the invasion of English words into the language and U.S.-style materialism into the Mexican value system. The U.S. accounts for most of Mexico's foreign trade and investment activities, but it is seen as a bully rather than a "good neighbor," a country that values "interests" over friends.

The fact that much of the U.S. Southwest (the states of Texas, New Mexico, Arizona, and California) was Mexican land 150 years ago is a continuing affront to Mexico's national pride. Mexico's dependence on U.S. trade, capital, technology, and aid, with strings attached, is a national humiliation. Mexicans are outraged by the poor treatment many of their compatriots must endure across the border. Moreover, they see some aspects of U.S. policy toward Mexico as disrespectful and aggressive interference in Mexico's internal affairs.

Mexicans have nothing against Canada or Canadians. Europeans are esteemed as *culto* (civilized, well-educated, enlightened). Though they recognize Spain's cultural contributions, the Mexican attitude toward Spaniards ranges from indifference to distaste for a people sometimes perceived as arrogant. Mexicans have little contact with people from Asia, the Middle East and Africa and have few preconceptions about them.

Gringo

The word *gringo* probably had its origins during the U.S.-Mexican War of 1848, when Mexicans exhorted invading U.S. troops in their green uniforms to go home ("green go"). Today, it is used to refer to any light-skinned foreigner, but particularly to those assumed to be from north of the border.

Many Mexicans call United States citizens *americanos*. Others see the use of "American" as an exclusive descriptor that is insulting — given that the citizens of North, Central and South America are all *americanos*. They prefer to call their neighbors *norteamericanos, estadunidenses...* or *gringos*.

Though some U.S. visitors feel offended by the latter term, it isn't always used pejoratively. (When in doubt, listen to the speaker's tone of voice.) *Gringo* may merely indicate the nationality or origin of a person or product, as in *es una marca gringa* (it's a *gringo* brand).

Beliefs about Foreigners

Common negative Mexican perceptions about people from other countries (especially the United States) include:

- They are in Mexico only for their own economic benefit.
- They are often very friendly but in an insincere, superficial way.
- They are loud, aggressive, impatient, inflexible, arrogant, and generally ill-mannered.
- Having grown up wealthy, they lack the strength of character that comes from hardship; as a result, they don't behave gracefully under pressure.
- They have poor morals and values, such as materialism, selfishness and wastefulness, and their women are promiscuous.
- They are optimistic, trusting and naive.
- They are not interested in learning about Mexico's history, culture or language.
- They look down upon Mexicans and believe their own culture and way of life are superior.

It should be noted these beliefs rarely interfere with a Mexican's genuine efforts to make non-Mexicans feel at home.

How Others View the Mexicans

Mexico is seen as a poor "Third World" country besieged by political corruption, low economic productivity and drug-related violence. The recent alleged involvement of the brother of ex-President Salinas in a high-level assassination, and the disclosure of his having amassed a fortune during his brother's administration, have reinforced Mexico's image abroad as a "narcodemocracy" — rife with nepotism and unscrupulous leaders who operate above the law. In addition, Mexicans are often thought of as being more romantic and volatile than practical and hardworking, and as suffering from a chronic "*mañana* mentality."

Mexicans also have a reputation for warmth and generosity, and these traits have gained them a place in the hearts of many North Americans and Europeans; the same is true for thousands of Latin American and Spanish exiles to whom Mexico has given a home. Cubans highly esteem Mexico as one of the few countries to stand by them during decades of U.S.-orchestrated ostracism.

Mexicans place great importance on how their country and how they, as a people, are seen by foreigners. They are highly insecure about their image abroad.

National Identity and Pride

Mexicans take great pride in their country's heritage. The city of Teotihuacán (Place of the Gods), which fell in 650 A.D., was larger than Rome at the height of its imperial glory. When the conquistadors arrived in the Aztec capital of Tenochtitlán in 1519, they found a dazzling metropolis laced through with canals, streets, botanical gardens, zoos, plazas, and elaborate temples that had been built without benefit of the wheel. It was, a Spanish chronicler wrote, more splendid than any city in Europe.

The ancient Mayans were the first civilization in the world to develop the mathematical concept of zero, and their calendar was more precise than some that are used today. Mexican foodstuffs, introduced to Europe by the explorer Cortez, included peanuts, sweet potatoes, tortillas, turkey, tomatoes, papaya and roasted cacao beans (chocolate).

Nationalism (*mexicanidad*) is instilled by the highly regulated educational system and constantly invoked by the government through patriotic appeals and the building of monuments. Every town has streets named after important events and heroes (*Independencia, Revolución, 16 de Septiembre, Juárez, Hidalgo*). TV and radio stations play the national anthem ("Mexicans, ready your swords and saddle to the call of war...") at the beginning and end of daily broadcasts.

Paisanos (countrymen) who have achieved international acclaim in the arts include the painters Diego Rivera, Frida Kahlo and Rufino Tamayo; the Nobel Prize-winning poet and essayist Octavio Paz, and novelist Carlos Fuentes. In the realm of popular culture, the comic actor Cantinflas, and the film stars Pedro Infante and Jorge Negrete are national icons (in death, as in life) beloved throughout the Spanish-speaking world.

In the political arena, there's Benito Juárez (a Zapotec Indian who became president of Mexico); Emiliano Zapata (leader of the "land and liberty" struggle in the 1910-1920 Mexican Revolution); and Lázaro Cárdenas (who, as president in the 1930s, seized the nation's oil fields from foreign companies and redistributed land to the poor on a large scale).

Other Mexican contributions to world culture include the development of a surgical technique for treating Parkinson's Disease; chemist Enrique Molina's research on the ozone cap, for which he received the Nobel Prize; the achievements of Fernando Valenzuela and other Mexican baseball players in the major leagues; and international prizes awarded to Mexico's Bohemia beer.

4 Cultural Stereotypes

A visitor's perceptions of Mexico may be based on personal experience, on what others have said or on stereotypes. These perceptions are almost certain to color both your social and business relationships. Those based on personal experience or valid research will probably be useful. Outdated or inaccurate information will create barriers.

While stereotypes about Mexicans vary, some are common.

Backward

Mexico is an underdeveloped land of peasants and poverty, tequila and mariachis, fiestas and siestas.

This enduring stereotype is based, in part, on Hollywood movies. It is nourished by the limited contact many people have with Mexico and Mexicans during vacations to tropical beaches, quick visits to border towns (thought of as emporia of cheap trinkets, cantinas, prostitution, and intestinal disturbances), and superficial interactions with immigrants and migrant workers in the U.S.

These images highlight Mexico's differences from the "First World" while concealing its similarities. They conjure up a "backward" land of rural poverty, border-town squalor and mass exodus, while overlooking the modern, dynamic, digitalized Mexico, with its sophisticated, Internet-linked professional sector and its large, urban middle class. They neglect the fact that most Mexicans live in culturally rich and historically fascinating population centers. These distortions focus on a lower standard of living while undervaluing such positive personal qualities as humor, warmth and generosity.

Mañana Mentality

Mexicans are lazy. They never do anything today that can be put off until a later date.

Things may not get done as rapidly in Mexico as in the "developed world." Worker productivity is lower and delays can be maddening for non-Mexicans and Mexicans alike. The so-called *mañana* (tomorrow) mentality suggests laziness and the lack of a work ethic; it judges Mexicans against foreign values.

Whereas some cultures promote a "time is money" ethos, most Mexicans value personal relations, family matters, and spontaneity more. They will miss work to take care of a sick child. Or they'll let a personal chat run its course rather than abruptly cut it off in order to "get back to work," which would be considered rude.

Outsiders may equate this relaxed attitude with irresponsibility or incompetence; Mexicans are likely to see people obsessed with getting things done ASAP as inflexible and slaves to the clock. Life is hard enough as it is. Why add more artificial pressures to it? Problems are to be faced patiently and one's time is to be enjoyed, not twisted into a struggle for optimal productivity.

Observers note that new telecommunications technologies and the growing focus on business efficiency have sped up the pace at which many things happen in Mexico. Still, unforeseen delays and resource scarcities are endemic in the developing world. Fighting "Mexican time" won't speed things up but only leave you frustrated.

Corrupt

Nothing gets done in Mexico without bribes and payoffs.

Corruption is rife in many aspects of Mexican life, from electoral fraud to diversion of funds by government officials, from payoffs for commercial concessions and contracts to *mordidas* ("bites") slipped to the police. Many outsiders view such practices with distaste or outrage. But these under-the-table transactions must be understood as outgrowths of economic and political realities. What would be considered bribery in the United States, for example, is often thought of as little more than a tip, an expeditious way of getting things done.

Incomes in Mexico are often grossly inadequate with 40 percent of the population living below the poverty line. According to government figures, only 12 percent of the workforce earns more than US$6,000 annually; most earn less than US$2,500. A traffic policeman's monthly salary may be less than US$200. Many Mexicans view *la mordida* as an improvised form of income redistribution. In commercial circles, it's often looked at as one of the costs of doing business. Bribes and gifts (in one form or another) grease the wheels of the economy and help many families make ends meet. Tax evasion not only buoys up the family economy but also keeps money out of the hands of officials (who are seen by almost everyone as hopelessly corrupt).

Most Mexicans do not like the pervasive graft, but they accept it. The practice is deeply ingrained and will not be wished away by moral codes preached from outside.

Anti-Gringo

Mexicans are hostile toward foreigners, especially people from the United States.

Most Mexicans have conflicting feelings towards their northern neighbor, ranging from suspicion and resentment to curiosity, admiration and envy. Still, as noted, Mexicans are by and large warm and welcoming to foreigners, willing to give them the benefit of the doubt.

Macho

Mexican men exhibit the worst aspects of being male.

Machismo, the aggressive projection of maleness, remains prevalent, especially among lower socioeconomic groups. It takes many forms, including womanizing, wife beating, boisterousness, extreme suspiciousness and jealousy, discouraging one's wife from working or having friends, being overly sensitive to real or imagined signs of disrespect from other men, and thinking of housework and childraising as women's work. In public, women often have to contend with *piropos* ("compliments") ranging from courtly to vulgar.

However, some Mexicans see *machismo* as including good qualities, such as a take-charge attitude, being a good provider, protecting one's loved ones from danger and a degree of stoicism. And many Mexican women contribute to the tradition, consciously or not, by giving their sons freedom while overprotecting their daughters.

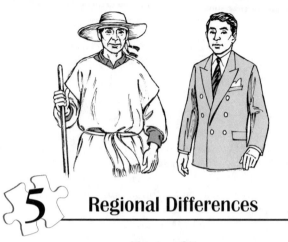

5 Regional Differences

Mexico City

The capital is the country's center of political power, industry and finance. Most multinational corporations doing business with Mexico have located their operations and/or headquarters here. Residents are known for being sharp and street-wise.

Though the economy is increasingly decentralized and national leaders pay lip service to transferring autonomy and resources to its states, many decisions must still be cleared (one way or another) through the capital. Mexico City's influence is felt — and often resented — in other parts of the country; the term *chilango* is sometimes used to refer to capital dwellers, who are perceived as overbearing and having a superior attitude.

West-Central Mexico

With Guadalajara at its hub, this is the nation's second leading commercial and financial center. Family enterprise, agriculture and ranching have traditionally dominated business here. Guadalajara's explosive growth in recent years has spurred its commercial sector to become increasingly sophisticated, especially among dynamic, medium-sized firms and affiliates of multinational companies (such as IBM and Kodak). Still, the atmosphere remains relaxed; the *tapatíos* (as the locals are called), though pigeonholed as right-wing and morally conservative, are also thought of as easygoing and fun-loving. Tequila and mariachis, symbols of *mexicanidad*, originated in this region.

Northern Mexico

Many of the country's largest industrial conglomerates and agribusiness farms (in Sinaloa and Sonora) are located here. In a region rich in mineral resources but with a rough terrain and harsh climate, the *norteños* (northerners) and *regiomontanos* (from Monterrey) see themselves as heirs to a hardy, pioneering tradition. They are known for having a strong work ethic, for industriousness and frugality, and for being more individualistic and straightforward than their compatriots. The standard of living is generally higher here than in the rest of the country.

Border Region

This is Mexico's fastest growing region. Migration to the U.S. and the proliferation of foreign-owned *maquiladoras* (in-bond assembly plants) have fueled the expansion and modernization of cities such as Tijuana, Ciudad Juárez and Matamoros. U.S. management styles have strongly influenced border-area business, creating an ambiance that mixes sophistication with the down-home horse-trading style found in the U.S. state of Texas.

Southern Mexico

Conservative *hacendados* (large landowners) with a colonial mind-set dominate Chiapas, the Yucatán Peninsula and other parts of the south. Business is based on class and paternalistic ties and is conducted at a very relaxed pace. Many of the indigenous inhabitants venture into the main-stream economy only to sell corn and crafts in local markets and to buy household implements.

Indigenous Peoples

Pure-blooded descendants of pre-Conquest Mexico can be found throughout the land. These include the Nahau and Otomi peoples (in the central plateau), the Tarascos (Michoacán), the Mayan peoples (Chiapas and the Yucatán Peninsula), the Tarahumaras (Chihuahua), the Zapotecs and Mixtecs (Oaxaca) and the Yaquis (Sonora).

Though millions of these men and women have left their traditional communities to seek better lives in the nation's cities (not to mention Los Angeles and New York), millions of others continue to live in relative isolation and speak their native tongues. The Huichols, for example, still maintain their ancient traditions, one of which is an annual trek across the Sierra Madre Occidental mountains to collect peyote (hallucinogenic cactus buds) for ceremonial purposes).

The current *zapatista* movement in Chiapas can be seen as an effort by indigenous peoples to acquire rights of citizenship (land, education, health care and legal protection, local autonomy) in order to preserve their traditional, agricultural way of life.

6 | Government & Business

Government Role in Business

The Mexican government's role in the country's economy has changed dramatically since the early 1980s. A centrally controlled economy based on protected domestic industry and oil exports has been both diversified and opened to market forces. Federal and state governments have aggressively pursued domestic and foreign investment, while promoting non-oil exports. These efforts have brought billions of dollars in capital to Mexico and helped expand foreign trade. Between 1982 and 1994, non-oil exports rose from 25 percent to 85 percent of total exports. Assembled and agricultural products have been key in the export diversification process.

Mexico's modernization drive has included government downsizing through the privatization of over 1,000 publicly owned enterprises. The current Zedillo administration has continued this process by seeking private management of ports and airlines and by putting the national railroad and parts of the formerly untouchable petrochemical monopoly on the auction block.

NAFTA

As the central strategy in opening up Mexico's economy, former President Carlos Salinas de Gortari actively pursued, negotiated, and in 1993 signed the North American Free Trade Agreement (NAFTA) with the United States and Canada. Known as *el Tratado de Libre Comercio* (*el TLC*) in Mexico, this pact gradually eliminates tariffs and other restrictions on the flow of goods, services and investment between the three countries.

The NAFTA-TLC created an economic bloc consisting of over 360 million consumers. It aims to enable more efficient use of North American resources (capital, land, labor and technology) and to stimulate market forces. It institutionalizes Mexico's economic reforms of the last decade and furthers the country's integration into the world economy — a priority since the mid-1980s. (Mexico joined GATT, which commits Mexico to open its economy to foreign competition, in 1986, and the World Trade Organization in 1994.)

Many Old Barriers Gone

The government has opened up previously closed sectors of the economy and most products are now subject to competitive pricing. Mexico's archaic landholding system has been overhauled. Meanwhile, government policy, combined with a glut in the labor market supply, have conspired to keep labor costs down. The minimum wage is US$3.89 a day in most of Mexico, though total labor costs are usually 40 to 80 percent higher.

Import permits are no longer needed for over 90 percent of all products. The previously Byzantine customs bureaucracy has been simplified. Full foreign ownership is now permitted in most sectors, and approval of foreign investments of up to $100 million has become automatic. New openings have been created for foreign banking, finance, insurance companies and retailers. The liberalization of franchising laws has sped the proliferation of domestic and foreign franchises in fast food and other services.

Another development conducive to trade is the modernization of Mexico's transportation infrastructure. A network of fast toll roads now expedite the two-way movement of goods between the U.S. border and central Mexico and between Mexican cities. Liberalized regulations have opened trucking and cargo handling to competition. Ports are being renovated. Updating of telecommunications systems and the end of *Teléfonos de México*'s (Telmex) monopoly have improved service and will lower costs.

Among the remaining significant barriers to trade and competition in Mexico are the concentration of wealth in relatively few hands, the high cost of borrowing, and the all-important role of *palancas* (connections). Those who lack *palancas* are severely restricted in the economic sphere.

Politics & Business = Bedfellows

At a 1994 dinner, President Salinas requested a US$25 million contribution from each of Mexico's 30 richest men as a way to strengthen the ruling party (the PRI). Though this appeal failed, the fact that it was even broached suggests the close alliance between politics and big business.

The government has continuously rewarded Mexico's magnates with lucrative contracts, concessions, subsidies, and by some accounts bargain basement prices for government-owned industries (for example, the privatization of banks, airlines

and Telmex). In the mid-1990s, a group of businessman from the northern state of Nuevo León
donated US$22 million to Ernesto Zedillo's presi-
dential campaign — a clear sign of big business'
interest in keeping the PRI in power.

No one knows how much of the nation's
wealth President Salinas appropriated during his
administration, but his brother managed to accu-
mulate an empire of real estate and commercial
properties and over US$100 million cash (which he
deposited in foreign banks under a pseudonym).
This is one high-profile example of the key role personal ties and loyalty play in the distribution and
concentration of wealth and power. Nepotism is
common — exemplified by politicians who lavishly
reward family friends and sometimes protect them
from the law.

Insiders

In terms of wealth and power, Mexico is one of
the world's most polarized countries. The economy
is smaller than that of the state of Florida, yet there
are more billionaires in Mexico than in any country
other than the U.S., Germany and Japan. Ten percent of the population owns 80 percent of the
nation's wealth — while over 40 percent of the population, about 40 million people, live below the
poverty line.

The Salinas administration's opening of the economy to competitive forces, and its selling of government enterprises to the private sector, accelerated the
enrichment of the rich and the impoverishment of the
middle and lower classes. Macroeconomic growth
came at the expense of the average Mexican's living
standard.

Foreign companies and speculators have also
become "insiders" in the Mexico of the 1990s. The

lowering of trade barriers, along with an overvalued peso, have led to a flood of imported consumer goods and services, often at the expense of small- and medium-sized domestic businesses. Dependence on short-term foreign investment (attracted by high interest rates), not for economic growth but to finance the balance of payments deficit, led to the peso's collapse in December 1994. The crisis that followed added billions of dollars to Mexico's already crippling foreign debt and imposed further "sacrifices" on a population already hard-hit by more than a decade of declining earnings.

A dramatic example of how policy has favored big business was the government's spending of billions of dollars (by some accounts, up to 10 percent of the GDP) to bail out the banking system in 1995. That same year, skyrocketing interest rates made it impossible for hundreds of thousands of Mexicans to make loan payments. Home foreclosures and auto repossessions were epidemic, and further borrowing (at variable interest rates of 60 to 100 percent) became prohibitive. El Barzón, a nationwide resistance movement of bank debtors, was (and continues to be, as of mid-1996) flooded with applicants. Members of El Barzón (the name refers to a farm oxen's yoke) make payments on the principal of their loans but refuse to pay interest.

An increase in the nationwide sales tax (*el IVA*) from 10 to 15 percent, coupled with a 50 percent inflation rate, severely curtailed buying power and economic activity. Tens of thousands of businesses closed and nearly a million workers lost their jobs — in an economy that needs to create a million new jobs per year to keep up with population growth.

7 The Work Environment

Today's stress on competitiveness and efficiency is gradually transforming the Mexican work environment. Yet customs in hiring, management and other aspects of what goes on in Mexican workplaces are often quite different from those found elsewhere in the West.

Nepotism

It's good to have an impressive resume, but even better if someone close to the boss recommends you. Company heads and managers like to surround themselves with people they know. Yet the concept of open competition is gradually catching on. In some Mexican cities, executive placement agencies now cater to the larger firms.

While hard work, productivity, educational training, merit and seniority are valued, promotions may depend more on cooperation, courtesy and faithfully carrying out an assigned task over a period of time. Moreover, family status plays a central role in many companies. Nepotism is a fact of life. Even though current economic pressures have forced austerity upon enterprises of all sizes, it is still common for family members to be brought aboard, whether or not they are really needed.

Job Protection

Mexico's labor force is abundant in young, unskilled labor and upper (but not middle) level managers. Some foreign investors are required to provide worker training as a precondition of investment approval. Those who do so should consider investing in worker benefit packages as well. New companies often lure these workers away with incentives that cost them considerably less than training does.

The labor laws are among the strongest in the world. A Mexican employer who wishes to dismiss someone must provide specific reasons and will suffer severe penalties if the situation is handled improperly.

Autocracy

Mexican businessmen — like technocrats, bureaucrats and male family heads — have a great respect and need for authority. Those below them in the hierarchy have been trained since childhood to defer to elders and other authority figures and to respect power and wealth.

In a traditionally organized firm, the *patrón* (boss) is unlikely to accept questioning from subordinates or seek their opinions. Nor does he grant them important decision-making power. Instead, they are given relatively limited, well-defined tasks to carry out more or less independently.

Due to the high value placed on hierarchical relationships, the Mexican worker or manager will attempt to guard his or her limited pocket of autonomy. He or she is likely to be efficient within this well-defined sphere but unlikely to display initiative. This dynamic often impedes teamwork. It's uncommon for co-workers to openly compete in an attempt to please superiors; such behavior is seen as treating one's co-workers rudely.

Most subordinates willingly submit to this highly centralized command structure for several reasons:

- To take initiative means to risk making mistakes and being punished for asserting too much independence.

- It's understood that jobs are relatively secure, and advancement most likely, for those who "don't rock the boat."

- The *patrón* has responsibilities to his employees as well as authority over them. For example, he can expect to be called upon to extend moral and material assistance to an employee's family. It is important for outsiders doing business in Mexico to be aware of this social (and occasionally financial) obligation.

A new generation of mostly U.S.-educated managers is beginning to have an influence. They believe in the decentralization of the decision-making process, increased delegation of authority and the encouragement of teamwork. But so far, their approach has made inroads only in the bigger cities and larger enterprises.

Traditional versus Modern

Communication between superiors and subordinates tends to be rigidly stylized. The superior may place more value on being in charge and being treated with deference than on initiative. The subordinate, in turn, is unlikely to share his thoughts about problematic procedures that come to his attention.

What is seen as monitoring in other countries is often seen as meddling in the Mexican work environment. So, out of respect for the subordinate's autonomy, the Mexican executive will leave the subordinate to carry out the task with little supervision. Likewise, the supervisor may be reluctant to provide corrective guidance, perhaps not wanting to imply that the subordinate is not performing his work adequately.

These patterns lead to a shortage of straightforward communication and lost opportunities to improve efficiency and productivity. Moreover, the lack of "meddling" and the formalized nature of communication can leave Mexican workers believing that the *patrón* doesn't like or trust them.

Non-Mexican businesspeople often find this system frustrating. But aggressive attempts to improve channels of communications and supervision by implementing foreign procedures run the risk of destroying the loyalty and trust of Mexican employees and managers. Suspicion and hostility toward outsiders may further hamper such efforts.

A more effective approach is to train new staff, gradually retrain those already in place, and make a concerted effort to personalize relations with both employees and business partners. Success in gaining respect and trust will lead to cooperation and hard work.

The Mexican Work Ethic

Working to live. In a culture where time is not reimbursed well in monetary terms, people work to live rather than live to work. Mexicans generally approach work as a necessary evil that provides the wherewithal to enjoy the more important things in life: family, friends and other earthly pleasures.

Family before work. The importance of family

life often has an impact on the working environment. It may lead, for example, to absences related to
illness in the family. Help wanted ads seeking secretaries, receptionists and shop clerks often specify
that candidates be single. This reflects the belief that
women who don't have children to care for are more
likely to be dependable workers. By contrast, married males are generally considered more responsible as employees than their single counterparts.

Fatalism. The sense of fatalism and powerlessness so characteristic of Mexican culture can play a
role in the workplace. Workers who feel that their
skills and initiative are not appreciated may conclude that the enterprise at hand is unimportant.
Foreign executives or managers are advised to be
careful not to label such an attitude as laziness. A
wiser approach would be to make Mexican
employees feel respected and appreciated; encour-
aging and rewarding initiative will lead to
employee trust, loyalty and consistent effort.

Hard workers. Aside from those employed by
the government or who hold white-collar jobs,
many Mexicans work six-day, 48-hour weeks. Mexicans' flexible attitude toward time translates into a
willingness to work after hours to get a job done,
particularly when issues of personal loyalty are
involved. Employers assume their employees will
put in extra hours to fill in for absent co-workers
and to carry out special assignments, often without
overtime pay.

In addition, economic hardship forces much of
the population to make considerable sacrifices.
During the current economic crisis, for example,
many employees have had to accept large wage
cuts rather than be laid off. Declining buying power
compels many Mexicans to work 12-hour shifts or
longer and to work more than one job.

8 Women in Business

Traditional Roles

Mexican women did not receive full suffrage until 1958. To a great extent, gender roles still follow traditional lines. In a prototypical home, the male family head is responsible for maintaining the family. The woman is in charge of child rearing, cooking, cleaning, hiring servants and allocating family funds. Surveys show that only about one of four Mexican husbands helps with housework; some spend a great deal of time outside of the home with friends and mistresses. Their wives are expected to be sexually faithful and devoted mothers.

Cultural beliefs, difficult-to-enforce laws, and women's economic dependence perpetuate this double standard. It's easier for a husband than a wife to be granted a divorce on the basis of infidelity. And many Mexican men get away with domestic violence and the failure to pay alimony or child support.

A notable exception to the above is the so-called matriarchy that has traditionally prevailed in the Tehuantepec Peninsula in the state of Oaxaca. Here, Zapotec Indian women play a dominant role in both local politics and the local economy. They have a reputation for "wearing the pants in the family" (though many dress in fantastically embroidered skirts), for loving to dance, and for being open about their sexual appetites. During certain local fiestas, amidst exploding firecrackers, brass band music and tolling bells, they climb up on church roofs and town hall balconies to pelt the men and boys below with candy, cakes, toys, mangoes, bananas (and, to add a touch of danger) pineapples and coconuts — a tradition known as *Tirada de Fruta*s (the "fruit throwing").

Women in the Workplace

In business and government, women generally hold support roles and are absent from decision-making positions. They continue to dominate such traditionally female occupations as schoolteaching, nursing, domestic work, and clerking in stores and banks. Statistics are telling:

- Less than one in 10 business owners and managers is female.
- Men earn, on average, 35 percent more than women.
- Only 40 percent of Mexican women have gone beyond primary school.

In the workplace, women are expected to display their femininity in the form of tight dresses or skirts, high-heeled shoes, careful hairdos and generous amounts of makeup. They are to be softspoken and nonaggressive in the company of men.

A secretary or receptionist's duties include serving coffee to her male boss. She is likely to receive a great deal of attention from male co-workers and superiors. But she lacks legal protection and in many cases must endure what would be considered sexual harassment in some other countries.

Changing Trends

Since 1970, the percentage of Mexican women who work outside the home has risen from 20 percent to over 40 percent. This is mainly due to declining family incomes and the fact that more and more women are single parents. It should also be noted that the number of women doctors, lawyers and university professors is increasing steadily.

Generally speaking, working women are seen as a necessary evil, a way to improve the "family economy." Many woman view wage-earning as a way to assert their independence from fathers and husbands (or at least to allow them discretionary spending money). But the concept of work as a means of "personal fulfillment" is not particularly common.

Strategies for Foreign Businesswomen

Non-Mexican businesswomen may need to adapt to certain cultural realities. It's inappropriate to criticize "inequities" in the workplace or to take a stand for women's rights. This will only create resentment and possibly harm your business prospects.

On the positive side, you will be treated with great courtesy by Mexican men with their old-school manners. They will take your calls, make time to hear what you have to say and go out of their way to be helpful.

One potential (though unlikely) drawback would involve having to interact with males who are not used to, or don't like, the idea of relating to women as equals. (This is particularly true among older men and those from working-class backgrounds). Poise, seriousness and competence are your best weapons for overcoming such resistance.

In advance communication with Mexican business contacts, a female team leader should make it clear that she's in charge by putting her name at the top of a list of team members. Before and during face-to-face meetings, she can ensure that her Mexican counterparts do not ignore her status by instructing her team members to defer all appropriate questions to her.

Be aware that Mexicans tend to think of women from the U.S. and Europe as promiscuous. You may find yourself in the company of men who assume that you're available simply because you're in Mexico without a male escort or your family.

Mexican women use various approaches to deflect unwanted advances. Yet foreign women not used to this kind of attention may find themselves in danger of wounding a sensitive male ego and damaging a business relationship. If you're in an uncomfortable situation, a calm, good-natured approach will best serve your interests. If it really becomes necessary, let your admirer know that you don't like his advances and would like them to stop.

Clothes that are considered innocuous in other countries may be taken as a sign of sexual advertising. To avoid misunderstandings, dress conservatively, particularly while conducting business or socializing with business contacts.

And be careful not to do anything that might offend a Mexican businessman's wife, such as attending a social event with him that she hasn't been invited to or isn't expected to attend. To provoke her jealousy or dislike might mean the end of your business relationship with her husband.

9   Making Connections

Cultivate Relationships

"Friendship and contacts," says an ex-U.S. consul who has lived and done business in Mexico for 40 years, "are the most valuable things in the mentality of the Mexicans."

Friends, relatives and colleagues help each other gain the needed information, advice and contacts. Businesspeople, government officials and others in advantageous positions tend to form networks of personal relationships that provide the *palancas* essential to getting new enterprises off the ground, attracting clients, obtaining contracts and cutting through red tape. The importance of personal relationships in business cannot be overemphasized. Who you know and who they know may count more than anything else.

Mexicans spend time over coffee or meals or drinks in order to get to know a potential associate and his or her intentions. They put as much stock in an individual's character as in their resources and expertise. Contracts may go to a friend or colleague rather than to the lowest bidder.

Cultivating these all-important relationships can be especially difficult for those unwilling to devote a great deal of time and energy to winning the trust of people who may be in a position to benefit them. This is not as cynical and manipulative as it may sound. It means developing genuine personal ties based on loyalty and reliability.

Once a foreign businessperson has been accepted into one of these old-boy interpersonal networks, his or her chances of establishing a successful business in Mexico will increase exponentially. Be aware that *palancas* are based on reciprocity — the balancing of favors received with favors given. When called on, you will be expected to go out of your way to use your own *palancas* to help others.

Go-Betweens

If you know someone who has done business in Mexico, consider asking them to make an introduction. If not, the Trade Commission of Mexico, which has offices in many countries, may be able to help you initiate contacts. (It can also keep you apprised of upcoming trade shows, where you can display your goods or services, gauge business prospects and pursue contacts).

Chambers of commerce and industry associations in Mexico are also potentially valuable resources. The American Chamber of Commerce has offices in Mexico City, Guadalajara and Monterrey, and most of its members are Mexican businesspeople. Another possibility would be to pay a business consultant to assist you.

Go to the Source

If none of the above works, consider taking a fact-finding trip to Mexico, where you can speak with people in your field firsthand. It's wise to call or fax first to inform specific people you want to meet who you are, why you would like to meet, and when you are going to be in town.

Another option is to arrange to visit a foreign-owned *maquiladora* (most are located near the Mexico-U.S. border). Executives at these assembly plants are usually happy to share their experiences and may be willing to help you make further contacts.

Patience and Respect

Mexican executives and managers devote a good part of each day to developing and maintaining business relationships, particularly when they're dealing with people they don't know. During your first set of meetings with your Mexican counterparts, expect to spend more time socializing than discussing substantive issues. Anticipate that working out the details of an agreement will require several trips to Mexico.

Remember that from the outset, the people with whom you are interacting will be evaluating you as a person, looking for traits valued in Mexico — dignity, respect, patience, flexibility, and seriousness coupled with a sense of humor. Though you may not see the point of long conversations and social events, they do. Let them set the pace at which the relationship develops.

A Mutually Beneficial Process

Learning about an associate will make communication and understanding smoother and help you decide how far to take the business relationship. Even if you end up not doing business with your contacts, you can count on them if a future need arises.

10 Strategies for Success

A history of having been taken advantage of by foreigners has made Mexicans suspicious of outsiders' intentions. Yet Mexico wants and needs foreign technology, capital goods, investment, trade, technical know-how and marketing expertise. Moreover, deregulation has promoted international commercial links and made Mexican businesspeople eager to establish cooperative ventures.

Though potential Mexican associates may be wary, they will treat you respectfully and give you a chance to win them over. A number of strategies will aid your endeavors.

Ten Golden Rules

1. **Find a matchmaker and "aim high".**
   Because personal ties are fundamental to Mexican business, it's to your advantage to have a third party put you in touch with those in positions to help you. Try to make contact with the highest levels of a Mexican company, where the power and decision-making are concentrated.

2. **Friendship before business.**
   Think of yourself as going to Mexico both to do

business and make friends. At the outset, focus on the latter. Let phone conversations, meetings, meals and social events flow at the pace set by your hosts. Don't expect to come home from the first or second trip with a deal. In subsequent visits, continue to take time to establish and strengthen relationships. If you do, you will win friends and allies and enhance your prospects; if you don't, you're likely to get involved in bad deals.

3. Show interest in Mexico.

Mexicans are flattered and honored when foreigners get to know and appreciate their country. Allow yourself time to see the sites. Show interest in Mexico's history and culture, its customs and cuisine. This will counteract the idea that foreigners are only interested in exploitation. If you are proficient in Spanish, so much the better.

4. Don't be an "ugly American."

The fastest way to alienate your Mexican counterparts is to barge into their country with a superiority complex. Being loud, demanding, condescending, or inflexibly insisting on having things your way won't win you a good reception. Being polite, friendly and easygoing will. Even if you spend 20 years in Mexico, you still might not understand some aspects of the culture; fighting practices that don't make sense to you won't change anything.

Take the attitude that you've come to learn from Mexicans, not criticize them. By keeping an open mind, you will encourage Mexicans to show you their best qualities: enthusiasm, warmth, hospitality and loyalty.

5. Be patient.

In most situations, losing your patience will be seen as losing your self-control. Expect delays to occur. If they don't, you will be pleasantly surprised.

Be careful not to convey impatience to your

Mexican counterparts through words or body language (sighs, hands on hips, looking at your watch), by interrupting or abruptly changing the subject. Such behavior will only work to your disadvantage. Relax. Exercise calmness and tact. Adopt the Mexican outlook that there is always time for humor, the unexpected, and to enjoy life.

6. Be polite.

You may never have the elegant manners that seem to come naturally to Mexicans, both young and old. And don't worry about what might be the "proper" behavior in any given situation. Rather, concentrate on being considerate toward others.

Use proper greetings and say "please" and "thank you." Avoid being abrupt, pushy or emphatically declaring "No," "I don't like that," or "I disagree." Above all, don't criticize or embarrass anyone publicly.

7. Show and command respect.

Respect is essential, particularly toward those in high positions. Call them by their titles. Thank and praise them when appropriate, without being obsequious, and they will respond in kind.

Keep in mind that foreigners will be evaluated not only by their manners but by their status and certain outward displays. Though it's not a good idea to brag about your accomplishments, let it be known if you are the head of your company or that you've earned a graduate degree. Providing favors useful to your counterparts can help you gain their loyalty and respect.

Being well dressed and neatly groomed are very important. Inappropriately casual dress may be construed as a sign of disrespect. Staying at a top-notch hotel will impress your Mexican counterparts, as will offering your guests a choice of upscale restaurants. But don't be ostentatious; it may be construed as flaunting your wealth, a sign of bad manners.

8. **Accept social invitations.**

If a Mexican invites you to his home, you have broken through formal barriers and are being honored with his trust. He is saying *mi casa es su casa* (my home is your home). Refusing such an invitation will be interpreted as a slap in the face. Show your thanks by bringing a gift and extending a reciprocal invitation.

9. **Make "win-win" propositions.**

Remember, Mexican businessmen will suspect non-Mexicans of wanting to take advantage, without showing any loyalty to Mexico or its people. Whatever your business, present it as a "win-win" proposition that will benefit both sides. The best way for it to be believed as such is for it to be so.

10. **Seek advice and help from people who know Mexico and Mexicans.**

Making contacts, finding out more about potential associates, strengthening relationships, negotiating successfully, dealing with bureaucracies, managing a business from day to day, and maintaining good relations with workers all require understanding of the differences between how things work in your country and how they work in Mexico. Each step of the way, identify and talk to experienced people who can help you understand the Mexicans and help you operate successfully. Many foreign companies have found using Mexican managers, accountants and other personnel to be the best approach.

Gift Giving

In Mexican business, gift giving plays a less critical role than in some cultures. A gift given prematurely may be viewed as an inappropriate attempt to short-circuit the elaborate courtship customary among potential associates. On the other hand, once you have forged a personal relationship, gifts can help reinforce it. If you give a personalized gift — one chosen based on your knowledge of the recipient's interests and tastes — your counterpart will recognize the thoughtfulness behind it. But be sure not to go overboard. Expensive items are fitting only for senior-level associates who have been instrumental to the success of a venture. Overdoing it may be taken as gauche or even insulting. And it may make the person feel compelled to reciprocate in kind.

Imported items such as scotch, brandy, cognac, foreign wine, cigarettes, and cheeses are appropriate gifts, so long as they are presented as novelties and not as superior to Mexican products. Electronic gadgets, pen and pencil sets, and lighters with your company's logo on it are other options. Toys for your counterpart's children are a welcome gesture. Likewise a scarf or perfume for secretarial personnel ("my wife sent this to you").

If you are invited to a Mexican home, gift giving is not strictly de rigueur, but your hosts will take kindly to a token of your appreciation. A bottle of hard liquor or wine, flowers, a plant, a cake, pastries, coffee table art books, crafts or another unusual item from your country, candy, or toys for the children are possibilities. Be aware that giving personal gifts to your associate's spouse may be misunderstood.

Wrap gifts simply. If you are given a gift and urged to open it in front of the giver, don't tear it open greedily.

11   Time

Mexicans are not as likely as people north of the border to "race against time" (their driving style notwithstanding), or to speak of "losing" or "wasting" time. They rarely cut short a social conversation because of an impending obligation. People take precedence over schedules. Mexicans are more likely to sacrifice a business opportunity than to lose a friend. And relationships are more important than the amount of time they take to develop.

Mexico's information infrastructure, lacking by First World standards, affects the pace at which things get done. Although improving at a dramatic pace, telecommunications can be difficult. Many of the smallest businesses and some private homes don't have telephones. The railway system is slow and under constant renovation. And although the highway network is expanding, some major roads remain in poor condition.

Appointments

Appointment times are somewhat fluid. In business, arriving a few minutes or even half an hour later than scheduled is considered perfectly acceptable. High-placed Mexicans may schedule more than one meeting at the same time, counting on some people to come late or not at all. (If someone has to wait, it reinforces the importance of the person being waited for.)

Schedule meetings between 10 A.M. and 1 P.M. or between 4 P.M. and 6 P.M. — hours when your counterpart is most likely to be in his office. Arrive promptly, but expect to wait for 30 minutes or more. Such delays are seldom intentional; bring a book or some work to keep yourself occupied.

If you are travelling by car to a destination in Mexico City, the chances are that you may not arrive on time for some appointments. You might offend someone but probably won't. Just apologize and say something came up (*algo sucedió*).

Social occasions may not begin until an hour after the designated time. Don't embarrass your host (who may not be ready) and yourself by arriving early.

Deadlines

Be aware that when Mexicans promise that a job will be ready by the time or date you request, there's a good chance they're saying so primarily to please (and not disappoint) you. Foreigners should take such an assurance as a "projection" rather than as a rigid commitment and plan accordingly.

Untimely delays are most prevalent in rural areas, public sector enterprises, and when dealing with excruciatingly slow-paced bureaucracies. Foreigners who need government forms and approvals should consider using a local Mexican intermediary or attorney who is familiar with procedures and personalities and has the *palancas* necessary to expedite such tasks.

12   Business Meetings

Preparation

Schedule the meeting about two weeks in advance, by fax or telephone. (Avoid the postal service. It can take three weeks for a letter to get from the U.S. to a big city in Mexico.) Let your counterpart choose the time and place. Confirm the appointment shortly before your departure for Mexico or soon after you arrive.

In advance, fax specific information on the nature of your business, how it might benefit the Mexican company, your position in your company, perhaps something about your prior experience and education, and the names and roles of others who will accompany you. You might also send brochures or other printed material on your company via a courier service.

The Meeting

Your initial meeting may occur in your counterpart's place of business. It will begin with handshakes and introductions; coffee and a snack may be served. Accept whatever is offered and at least make a pretense of tasting it. In some larger, big-city corporations, this home-style, non-optional hospitality is disappearing.

Let your counterpart direct the course of the conversation. You will likely be asked how long you have been in Mexico and what you have done so far. This is an opportunity to show your interest in Mexican culture as well as business. When you present your business, keep it general: what you are interested in doing and its potential mutual benefits. The calmer you are, the better the Mexicans will receive you. Don't speed things up by going into much initial detail. If what you are proposing seems mutually beneficial and the personalities involved are compatible, the specifics will follow at a later date.

You may receive a charmingly friendly (though formal) reception. If your host seems vague and indirect, he's probably sizing you up and trying to decipher your intentions. Don't worry. Use this opportunity to observe what you can about the people and company you are dealing with, and try to determine who has the most influence and decision-making power.

Avoid getting impatient with small talk or annoyed by interruptions. If you are part of a team, save comments among yourselves for after you've left your counterparts' presence. Mexicans find private asides disrespectful and rude.

Executive Meals

Many initial business contacts occur in restaurants and bars. These are relaxed events, more social than business-oriented, though spouses are not generally invited. Substantive business matters should not be brought up unless your Mexican host introduces the topic.

Appropriate topics of discussion include general business and economic issues, world news, sports, and family and mutual acquaintances. Catty gossip is considered in bad taste, as is talk about money at this early stage. Avoid sensitive issues like politics, religion, corruption or U.S.-Mexican relations. Don't display bad taste by repeating former U.S. President Carter's infamous public comment about his bout with "Montezuma's Revenge" (dysentery) at a Mexican state dinner.

Breakfast meetings usually take place in a U.S.-style coffee shop. Though considered more intimate than lunch meetings, they are sometimes reserved for matters of lesser importance.

Lunch meetings are often used to strengthen personal bonds and business ties, to finalize deals, or to celebrate an agreement. Lunch is the main meal of the day and usually begins in mid-afternoon. Be prepared for it to last two hours or so.

Evening business meals are less common and usually connote a more personal contact. Such events seldom begin before 9 P.M. and can sometimes last until the early hours of morning.

13 Negotiating with the Mexicans

Preparation

Before the formal meeting, give your Mexican counterparts a detailed written explanation of the issues to be discussed. Include a list of who will be attending, along with their titles and responsibilities, and ask the Mexicans to respond in kind. State the format you wish to follow and ask if they have any objections.

It's crucial to clarify in advance the issue of authority. Get a clear idea of the discretionary power of those with whom you will be negotiating. Be certain that you are dealing with people who have decision-making authority. At the very least, know which Mexican team member will communicate with the top and how quickly approval can be obtained.

Formulating an Approach

A positional bargaining approach is not usually the most effective method of negotiating in Mexico, for several reasons:

- Your counterparts have carefully assessed your character and interests before deciding to enter into negotiations.

- Using your company's superior size and financial strength to pressure the other side into accepting an agreement on your terms may backfire, causing them to withdraw from the negotiations or to not perform according to the contract's terms.

- Taking an uncompromising approach without paying attention to the personal aspects of the transaction is unwise. If the Mexicans don't accept you as a person, they will feel no obligation to treat you fairly.

Formulate a "win-win" approach that satisfies both sides' interests and demonstrates your goodwill throughout the negotiating process.

Beginning the Meeting

Negotiations are likely to be held at a hotel, conference center, or meeting room near the Mexican place of business. If you have a preference for a particular place, it's acceptable to ask your counterparts to arrange to meet there.

Mexican subordinates usually arrive early to attend to seating arrangements and other details. A higher status executive arrives later, accompanied by a personal secretary, interpreter and perhaps a bodyguard. He may have others in his entourage, though it's considered bad form to pack the room with non-essential retainers. This grand entrance makes it clear who the power broker is.

The first few minutes are devoted to pleasantries, with senior people taking the lead. Efforts to immediately tackle the business at hand will be construed as rushed, rude and suspicious. Remember that Mexicans see impatience as one of the main failings of non-Mexicans. Easing into substantive issues gives both sides time to feel comfortable with each other.

The Negotiation

The head of the host side usually opens the meeting with formal welcoming remarks. He then turns the floor over to the head of the guest delegation. The visitors' team leader should begin by reiterating the previously agreed-upon agenda and structure of the meeting. Distributing an outline or using an overhead transparency can clarify issues to be covered. The Mexican team will respond item by item.

From this point on, the negotiations take on a life of their own. It is up to each side to stay focused and address each issue thoroughly. But be flexible. Don't insist on sticking adamantly to the agenda if all the relevant points are being covered. Remember that decisions in Mexico are based as much or more on context and personal chemistry as on content. And expect your counterparts to bargain (*regatear*). Mexicans are apt to see those who don't play the give-and-take game as naive and lacking in social skills.

Don't let the interaction turn into a confrontation. Keep lines of escape open. If it becomes apparent that agreement cannot be reached on key issues, the talks should be permitted to fade away quietly rather than end on a note of dramatic conflict. This allows everyone to save face and preserves the possibility of future talks.

Top Six Mexican Tactics

1. Deference to principal negotiator and close team unity, making it impossible to exploit differences among team members. Participation by other team members is often limited to narrow technical issues.

2. Emphasis on people skills make negotiators very experienced and persuasive.

3. Attempts to play on friendship to obtain concessions.

4. Pressure exerted according to assessment of how badly the other side wants the agreement.

5. Exploiting outsiders' sense of impatience, urgency.

6. Use of temper to soften counterparts up.

Tips for Foreign Negotiators

- Be thoroughly prepared. Interview other businesspeople who have dealt with your counterparts. Study existing contracts they have entered into and know the professional history of their personnel.

- Ask yourself, "If I were representing their team, what would I ask for? What would be a fair agreement?" Use this perspective to make a list of possible positions the other side may take and to develop alternatives before coming to the negotiating table.

- Develop a best-alternative position but don't let your counterparts know what it is. If necessary, use it as a bargaining tool.

- Use objective criteria when formulating your proposal. Citing independent market studies, government price indexes and other impartial measures will make it difficult for the other side to contest your position on emotional or anecdotal grounds.

- Remain calm no matter what happens. Composure and self-control will work in your favor.

- Emphasize the shared benefits of the proposed venture. Reassure the Mexican team that you are thinking long-term and want to satisfy mutual concerns.

- Play your cards one at a time, not all at once. This fits well with the Mexican viewpoint of negotiation as a social transaction. It also avoids a take-it-or-leave-it approach, which is likely to be constructed as demanding, insulting, and not "playing the game."

- Listen carefully and take detailed notes. To dispel confusion and misunderstanding, repeat important points and ask for clarification.

- Don't force yes-no declarations. Questions that may require a negative response clash with the Mexican cultural tendency to answer "yes," "maybe" or "we'll see" out of politeness. Phrase questions that allow your counterparts to indicate a tendency rather than a direct answer. Follow up by eliciting additional information to help you determine how strong that tendency is.

- Be slow and methodical. Impatience is a weakness the Mexicans can exploit. You might suggest a willingness to postpone your return home or make a second trip if differences cannot be settled this time.

- Saying the least can get you the most. Sitting quietly for what seems like an eternity gives the appearance of serious pondering and avoids hasty responses. Your silence may result in the other side coming out with additional information or concessions.

- Build in contingent agreements detailing penalties for non-performance. If the Mexican team objects, tell them that you do not doubt their goodwill and that such addenda are mere formalities demanded by your lawyers.

- Allow yourself the freedom to walk out if you feel you aren't getting what you need. Bad business is worse than no business. One observer estimates that every one-on-one contact you have influences 30 or 40 of that businessperson's *socios* (associates).

Interpreters

Those who have to speak a foreign language during high-stakes negotiations are at a disadvantage. The members of most large Mexican firms are proficient in English. However, unless your team includes someone who communicates fluently in Mexican Spanish, you may need to employ the services of a competent interpreter. Don't depend on the person who interprets for the other side. Though that person probably won't try to mislead you, he or she may miss the nuances of your language.

Tips on Using Interpreters

1. Establish guidelines.

Before a meeting, plan the mechanics of how you will work together, such as how long you should speak before pausing for interpretation. Go over any specialized vocabulary, brief him thoroughly, and allow time for him to become familiar with your style, humor and body language, so that he can accurately convey your messages.

2. Address your Mexican counterpart.

Speak to the head of the Mexican team, not to the interpreter. Mexicans value personal communication. But be careful not to "talk down" or speak more loudly than necessary, and avoid using idiomatic expressions and slang.

3. Don't exhaust your interpreter.

Stop every couple of sentences to allow for interpretation, and try to limit each sentence to one main point. Interpreters need to rest at least every two hours. Be aware that using an interpreter can stretch a meeting to three times its normal length.

4.   Emphasize important points as they arise.

Abstract and complicated discussion is seldom directly translatable. You can help ensure that important points get across by repeating or emphasizing them and by making certain that your verbal and non-verbal (body language) messages are consistent with each other.

5.   Review what's been said and anticipate what's coming.

After a meeting or during breaks, review with your interpreter the main points that both sides have made. Ask what he or she observed about the other side's position or behavior. Try to get a feel for the direction in which negotiations are headed, and anticipate what will need to be said later on.

Contracts, Mexican-style

Be aware that a difference may exist between what seems to be an honest verbal or written promise and the actual intention or ability of the contracting party to perform. For example, your Mexican counterpart may consider time commitments as more flexible than you do.

Mexicans tend to enjoy developing projects, but they often have less interest in the detail work needed to implement and administer them. The lack of delegated authority and the shortage of sophisticated management tools can lead to frustration, apathy and unmet goals.

When entering into a cooperative venture, foreign businesspeople might suggest there be built-in bilateral cooperation between mid-level managers and technicians. If the suggestion is made tactfully, foreign managers may be able to monitor progress and influence outcomes. Another strategy would be to build rigorous progress reporting into the agreement.

Be aware that Mexico has only recently begun to institute the rule of law in business; many executives still view written contracts as of secondary importance to personal commitments between associates. Consult with a local attorney about the legally binding nature and enforceability of any written or verbal agreements you make. Also be aware that judicial relief is extremely time-consuming, costly and uncertain — reason enough to work out potential conflicts ahead of time.

Keep in mind that, from a Mexican perspective, coming to an agreement with you makes you part of their close, personal network of business associates. It's crucial that you be comfortable with both the benefits and responsibilities of this network.

14 Business Outside the Law

Evading the Tax Man

Government surveys suggest that up to 40 percent of the work force may make their living through employment outside the tax system. If taken into account, this informal economy would add 25 to 40 percent to the GNP.

Perhaps the most visible of these "un-taxed" activities are *los tianguis* (street markets), which sell everything from fresh produce to *fayuca* (contraband). (It's estimated that in recent years, U.S. film, music and software industries have lost $485 million annually to Mexican pirates, thus violating NAFTA's tough copyright standards.) Millions of other Mexicans work as "paid under the table" housekeepers and gardeners, sell door to door, set up taco stands each evening, convert their driveways into diners, wash windshields at intersections, and sing on buses and in cantinas.

Such tactics are considered survival strategies; the government estimates that 80 percent of the about one million Mexicans who enter the job market each year will be unable to find employment in the formal economy. Then too, legitimate businesses avoid paying taxes (and abiding by labor laws) by underreporting sales and hiring undocumented workers.

Graft and Corruption

It's not uncommon for a driver to slip a few pesos to a traffic cop to avoid having his or her license confiscated; the option is to have to wait in line to pay a similar or higher fee to the local motor vehicle office. Though many Mexicans detest the *mordida* custom, and though the government vows to end it, it is still more the rule than the exception. Those who accept (and even request) bribes consider them a necessary evil, given the generally low state of Mexican salaries.

Entrepreneurs sometimes resort to giving a bureaucrat money or a gift in order to cut through the red tape involved in opening a new business, winning a contract, or slipping past building codes, environmental regulations and tax auditors. Mexican presidents, governors, mayors and others with access to public funds have long participated in large-scale graft, and many have left office rich men.

In general, Mexicans consider politicians and police to be venal and untrustworthy and *los judiciales* (equivalent to the FBI in the U.S.) to be particularly corrupt, if not dangerous. It's well known that many *judiciales* are in the employ of drug lords, and rumors about ties between high-level politicians and drug traffickers are often in the news.

Songs of Drugs & Heroes

Drug smuggling in northern Mexico (cocaine, heroin and marijuana) is so lucrative that it has inspired its own music, the *narco corrido*. These ballads, which romanticize the exploits of men on the wrong side of the law, are sold as cassettes but can also be heard on local radio stations. Not only has drug money improved any number of local economies, but some drug lords have endowed their hometowns with hospitals and schools. The rags-to-riches success of those in the trade is a popular *narco corrido* theme. One tune tells the true story of El Guëro Palma, a drug honcho who was captured by the police after his Lear jet crashed. The song begins with Palma telling his pilot to be brave as the plane goes down and ends with a warning that Palma's jail days may soon be over. "Don't feel smug, *señor*...Your pillows just might explode. For the king lives on."

Art Fakes

Phony pre-Hispanic ceramics — statuary, masks, bowls and the like, supposedly fashioned by ancient Aztecs, Mayans and others — have long been a source of revenue. While some pieces are crude, others are convincing enough to fool even sophisticated collectors. Brigido Lara, a contemporary Mexican art forger (and now a professional fake buster) was single-handedly responsible for creating almost an entire civilization's worth of objects from the Veracruz classical period.

Present Changes and Future Outlook

Crackdowns typically come at the beginning of new administrations, with "a big fish" singled out as an exampl. But no one really believes that a significant anti-crime campaign is under way; most see Mexico's autocratic political system and its economic corruption as inseparable. The fact that PAN (*Partido de Acción Nacional*), an opposition party, has won four state (and numerous local) governorships in recent years represents an undeniable crack in the PRI's 70-year monopoly of power.

Names & Greetings

Mexicans sometimes have two surnames and always have two given names. In the case of Juan Manuel Anaya Zamora, for example, Juan and Manuel are both given names. The surname Anaya comes from his father. Zamora is his mother's maiden name.

When a woman marries, she replaces her mother's last name with her husband's. So when Isabel Vásquez Fernández marries Jorge Del Valle, she becomes Isabel Vásquez de Del Valle; "de" stands for "wife of." Their children's surnames will be Del Valle Vásquez.

Forms of Address

Mexicans introduce themselves using their given name and either one or both surnames (and may add *para servirle* or *á sus ordenes*, meaning "at your service"). When addressing someone formally, they use only the other party's first surname: for example, *Buenos dias, Señor Anaya*, or *Buenas tardes, Señora Vásquez*.

If you're not sure how to pronounce someone's name, don't hesitate to ask, and don't make the mistake of addressing or referring to someone by their second surname. For correspondence or on legal documents, use the person's entire name.

Spanish contains formal (*usted*) and familiar (*tú*) forms of address, and each employs different verb forms. The formal mode is appropriate when subordinates address superiors, when people speak to strangers or to their elders, and for men and women who don't know each other well. People of equal professional and social standing, as well as family members, generally address each other with familiar forms.

Common Mexican Business Titles

In both business and government, *Licenciado* is a catch-all title that acknowledges a person's qualifications. Technically, it refers to someone who holds a university degree, but there may be more *licenciados* in Mexico than university graduates. Other titles appropriate to a person's profession include *Doctor, Ingeniero, Arquitecto* and *Profesor*. Female forms have an "a" at the end: for example, *Doctora, Arquitecta or Licenciada*.

Note: Conventional practice is to address all female office personnel (other than executives), shop workers and waitresses as *Señorita*, regardless of their age or marital status.

Other titles include *gerente* (manager), *subgerente* (assistant manager), *director de mercadotecnia* (marketing director), *jefe de ventas* (sales manager), *agente de ventas* (salesperson), *contador* (accountant) and *abogado* (attorney).

Greetings

A normal greeting when dealing with someone of equal status in a business setting includes a handshake and a friendly smile. If this is a first meeting, hand out business cards, preferably printed in both your language and Spanish. In a social event at someone's home or in a restaurant, take the time to individually greet each person, even if this means shaking 25 or 30 hands.

If a Mexican business associate greets you or says good-bye with an *abrazo* (hug) — by grabbing your arm or putting his arm around your shoulder and punctuating it with a couple of claps on the back — it's a signal that you've begun to gain his trust. Don't insult him by shying away from such contact.

In addition to shaking hands, women often make cheek-to-cheek contact and sometimes kiss an established acquaintance of either sex on the cheek, even in a business setting. Non-Mexican businesspeople should accept and return such a greeting.

Farewells

Mexican good-byes involve the same hand-shakes, *abrazos* and/or kisses, but they may be more drawn out. At a social event, a good-bye that begins in the living room may continue as the host or hosts accompany the guests outside and to their automobiles. Half an hour later, they may still be chatting. The farewells will be repeated before the guests get into their cars and will involve such parting phrases as *que te vaya bien* (I hope things go well for you), *hasta luego* (see you later) or *nos hablamos* (we'll talk). *Buenas noches* is both a greeting and a good-bye. As a foreigner, do not gloss over these pleasantries when taking your leave.

16 Communication Styles

In Mexico, much interpersonal communication takes place below the surface. While words themselves are important, the implicit attitudes behind them are even more so. The following are common traits of the Mexican communication style:

- A great deal of polite, even obsequious, formality is employed at the outset of interactions to acknowledge unequal status (such as subordinate-superior or client-patron), communicate respect, and also to keep others at a distance.

- In business communication among equals, the formality is relaxed once the appropriate mutual respect has been shown and the relationship has progressed to a more personal level.

- Mexicans strive to hide negative feelings and avoid direct confrontation.

- Words are often chosen for the sake of politeness and a desire to not offend, rather than in the interest of clear communication. Generally, Mexicans find it preferable to say "yes," "maybe" or "we'll see," even if they mean "no."

- Mexicans tend to analyze someone else's words carefully, looking for why they were said and what was really meant.

Ten Golden Rules

The following will help you become more aware of how your body language and emotions may be interpreted in Mexico.

1. Don't avoid body contact or eye contact.

Foreign men not used to conversing in close proximity or being touched or hugged by other men may feel uncomfortable with these customs. But once you've begun to develop a personal relationship, "keeping your distance" may be interpreted as unfriendliness. Learn to accept these Mexican traditions in order to avoid sending the wrong message. Likewise, shying away from eye contact, whether in a social or business context, may be construed as suspicious behavior.

2. Don't show impatience.

Repeatedly glancing at your watch, putting your hands on your hips or other physical signs of impatience may alienate your Mexican counterparts. They may assume that you consider it more important to keep to your schedule or get things done efficiently than to interact with them.

3. Speak softly.

Keeping the volume and tone of your voice under control are reflections of both personal dignity and good manners. And they will help contradict the "ugly American" stereotype (regardless of your nationality). Don't speak too softly, however; whispering in front of others is considered rude.

4. Be aware of your posture.

Slouching, leaning against walls, leaning back in your chair and other relaxed postures may be construed as sloppiness or a lack of concern for how others perceive you. Be especially careful to avoid standing with your hands on your hips, which may be interpreted as an aggressive or challenging posture.

5. Let your host take the lead.

Allow your Mexican host or hosts to set the tone, content and pace of interactions. Observe and follow what seems to be appropriate behavior in a given circumstance.

6. Listen more — talk less.

Listen patiently and let people finish talking before you speak. If you don't understand what has been said, ask for it to be clarified.

7. Be tactful.

Except among family members, Mexicans rarely directly express disagreement or negative sentiments. Find an indirect, diplomatic way to express disagreement or dislike. If it's necessary to convey displeasure to someone, do so gently and in private.

8. Stay calm at all costs.

Mexicans are adept at displaying calm and diplomacy under pressure. If you feel frustration or anger rising within you, suppress it. Always seek an amicable way to soften or avoid open conflict.

9. Don't insult people.

Mexicans are highly sensitive to perceived disrespect. Don't give them reason to feel suspicious or hostile toward you. If you are unhappy about some aspect of their behavior, find a way to tactfully appeal to them for what you want without being demanding or sarcastic.

10. Keep your dignity.

Overly informal behavior may be seen as undignified for someone in a position to command respect. Maintain a balance between warm communication and mutual respect, between friendliness and dignity.

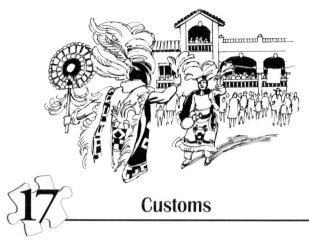

17   Customs

Fairs and Festivals

Mexico is a land of colorful street markets and a wide variety of festivals. *El Festival Cervantino*, named after Miguel de Cervantes (the 16th century author of the novel *Don Quixote*), draws an international gathering of theater groups, musicians, artists and craftspeople every autumn. *Carnaval* fills the streets of Veracruz, Mazatlan and other cities with parades, singing and dancing each February.

El Día de Los Muertos (Day of the Dead) blends the indigenous tradition of honoring the dead with the Catholic All Souls Day. On November 2nd, family members set up altars of marigolds, candles and food offerings in memory of deceased relatives, school groups build altars to honor cultural and historical figures, and cemeteries become picnic grounds for the day.

Each city, town and village has a festival dedicated to the local patron saint, replete with processions, fireworks and street vendors selling everything under the sun. During the Day of the Virgin of Zapopan, over a million faithful form a four-mile procession from Guadalajara's cathedral to the basilica in Zapopan. Some pilgrims ride in

from the countryside on horseback; others fly in
from California, New York and beyond.

Traditional Dances

There are hundreds of them, and many are of
pre-Hispanic origin. *Moros y Cristianos* re-enacts the
Christians' victory over the Moors in medieval
Spain. Indigenous dancers in Puebla don enormous
feathered headdresses to honor the sacred quetzal
bird. The Totonac Indian *voladores* ("flying men") of
Papantla, Veracruz, attach a rope to one leg and
swing down from the top of 20-meter-high poles.
And Mexico City's *Ballet Folklórico* performs traditional Mexican dances for audiences around the
world.

Artesanía

The tradition of Mexican craftsmanship pre-
dates the Spanish Conquest. Later, indigenous
craftsmen lent their skills to the building and orna-
menting of baroque churches across the land.

Some Mexican *artesanía* (handicrafts) are inter-
nationally recognized: Taxco silver jewelry; Oax-
acan hand-loomed rugs; embroidered blouses and
woven handbags from Chiapas; blown glass items
and ceramics from the Guadalajara area; fountains
cut from a native stone called *cantera*; rustic
wooden furniture; work in copper and tin; a color-
fully painted cousin of Chinese porcelain known as
talavera; hand-tooled leather goods; and a vast
array of pottery and tiles.

Mexicans have a special affinity for combining
the practical with the decorative and for transforming the ordinary into the extraordinary through the
use of vibrant color.

18 Dress & Appearance

Traditional Attire

Traditional dress is more evident in Diego Rivera's murals and Frida Kahlo's self-portraits than in the wardrobes of most Mexicans today. Visitors hoping to see colorful hand-embroidered dresses or the broad straw hats and rough-hewn *huaraches* of Mexican *campesinos* (peasant farmers) will have their best luck attending folkloric dance presentations.

In everyday life, *huipiles* (loose embroidered shifts), *fajas* (waist sashes) and *rebozos* (shawls) are sometimes worn by indigenous women and university students in big cities. Woolen tunics and *serapes* are worn by males in some indigenous communities in the south, and cowboy hats and pointed boots remain standard garb for men in rural areas and small towns.

Contemporary Styles

The indigenous peoples of Mexico were horrified by the Spanish conquistadors' stench and their custom of not bathing regularly. Today help-wanted ads often specify that only people with *buena presentación* should apply. To be less than neatly dressed and groomed is considered a lack of respect for oneself, and for others as well.

Upper-class Mexicans dress to project status and wealth. There is little "dressing down," though overly flashy or faddish clothing is generally avoided as being too "extravagant."

Formality takes precedence over comfort, even in Mexico's tropical regions. In business settings, men should wear ties and dark suits. Expensive but understated accessories make a good impression. However, in small towns and rural areas, where ties and other symbols of big-city wealth may be seen as pretentious, a sport coat, dark slacks and dress shoes are formal enough.

Women should wear conservative hemlines and necklines. Though secretaries often wear mini-skirts, female executives do not. Revealing clothing is appropriate only at resorts. Pants are acceptable for women in informal situations. Mexican women pay a lot of attention to their hair and makeup, regardless of the occasion, but don't feel that you have to conform to the heavy, vivid use of makeup that is common.

Nights are rarely cold anywhere in Mexico; medium weight coats are usually sufficient in winter. If you're traveling during the rainy season (June through September), bring an umbrella and light raincoat.

Most Mexicans think it's childish for men to wear shorts or tennis shoes, except at the beach or while playing sports. They are mystified as to why anyone would choose to wear cut-offs in public or take the liberty of kicking off their shoes in someone else's home.

19 Reading the Mexicans

Mexicans are often so formal and guarded that it's hard for them to figure each other out. Asking directly what someone thinks, feels or intends to do may not help; standards of politeness may further cloud the truth. This deciphering can be even more difficult for outsiders, especially those accustomed to taking words at face value and being able to read people's sentiments clearly.

A few clues may help you better understand the subtleties:

- During an initial contact, you may encounter vagueness, indirectness, or even an excess of silence. These are most likely delaying tactics used in order to size you up.

- If someone who previously lowered his guard with you raises it again by suddenly becoming very formal, you may have offended him in some way or lost his trust. You might ask if this is the case, but don't expect a direct answer.

- Be aware that "yes" may not mean yes and that "maybe" may mean no. You may have to ask further questions to pin down your counterpart's true meaning. Use a good-natured approach.

- When asking for directions, be skeptical about the information you get. Some Mexicans are apt to tell you how to get somewhere rather than disappoint you (or seem ignorant) by saying that they don't really know.

Common Gestures and Expressions

- Shaking the hand from side to side with the palm facing forward and only the index finger extended means "no."
- A flip of the head upward and a raising of the eyebrows signal an informal greeting or good-bye.
- "*Salud*" is used after someone sneezes and to make a toast.
- The versatile "*Ay*" (pronounced "ayeee") expresses surprise, pain, admiration, and sometimes distaste.
- Forming a circle with your index finger and thumb doesn't mean "okay." It's an obscene gesture.
- Some men cross their legs at the knee while sitting. Others think this position is suitable only for women and homosexuals.
- Never point at anyone.
- It's undignified to summon a waiter by making a "pssst" sound or by snapping your fingers.
- Throwing something to another person instead of handing it to them is ill-mannered.
- When paying for something, put the money into the cashier's hand. If you put it on the counter, it may appear that you don't want to touch the person.

20 Entertaining

Mexican Food

The Mexican food usually served in other countries is a limited and somewhat bland version of the original. *Enchiladas* are best categorized as "Tex-Mex," since they originated in Texas and the far northern region of Mexico. *Nachos* and *chimichangas* are American inventions. And you won't find *burritos* (although in the north, there's something similar, called a *burrita*).

Genuine Mexican cuisine blends indigenous foods (corn, beans, tomatoes and dozens of types of chile peppers) with the meat, dairy products and chicken introduced by European colonists. Examples of this gastronomic mingling include *birria* (a spicy goat stew) and *mole* (a bold sauce of chile peppers, chocolate, tomatoes, herbs, spices, nuts, and sesame or pumpkin seeds, usually eaten over turkey or chicken). The story goes that Dominican nuns in 17th-century Puebla created *mole* when they had to throw something together from a denuded larder to impress the visiting Viceroy. *Guacamole* is mashed and seasoned avocado, often served as a dip.

Salsa — made of tomatoes, garlic, cilantro and

chiles (spicy-hot peppers) — accompanies most meals. *Chiles* come in dozens of varieties (such as *habañero, serrano, jalapeño* and *poblano*) and are consumed in hundreds of ways. Venison is a specialty in some areas; *mariscos* (shellfish) and *tortuga* (turtle) are popular, particularly along the coasts. *Ceviche* is a raw seafood cocktail marinated in lime and spices.

Soups range from *sopa de ajo* (garlic with egg yolk) to *flor de calabaza* (squash blossom), from *gazpacho* (chilled vegetable) to *caldo tlalpeño* (a spicy broth with garbanzos, avocado, shredded chicken and rice). *Menudo,* a popular tripe soup, features the spiced insides of various four-legged creatures. Some of Mexico's more unusual fruits include *guayaba* (guava), *tuña* (prickly pear cactus fruit), *zapote* (from the chicle tree) and *cherimoya* (custard apple).

Cinnamon, clove, and pepper sailed to Mexico aboard the Manila galleon and found their way into another imaginative convent creation: *chiles en nogada*. When Agustín de Iturbide, Emperor of Mexico, came to visit after the War of Independence (circa 1823), Augustine nuns welcomed him with long, thin *poblano* chiles stuffed with a spicy-sweet chopped-meat *picadillo*, topped with a walnut cream sauce and sprinkled with pomegranate seeds.

Mexican Drinks

Montezuma and his nobles enjoyed frothy jugs of a beverage made from vanilla (a member of the orchid family) and roasted cacao beans (chocolate). *Atole,* a warm, corn-based drink, was also common in the royal Aztec court. Whip chocolate into atole and you get *champurrado. Tejuino,* also from the indigenous past, blends fermented corn, lime juice, and crushed ice with a more recent invention — sherbet.

Aguas frescas are typically made of fresh seasonal fruit blended with water and ice; variations include tamarind, *jamaica* (hibiscus flowers), *cebada* (barley) and *agua de horchata* (rice). *Café de olla* (coffee brewed with cinnamon and raw sugar) is served in many restaurants.

Domestically made alcoholic beverages include *tequila*, rum, brandy, kahlua (a coffee-based liquor) and beer. Several of the latter have won international taste awards. *Tequila* is distilled from blue agave, which grows in and around the town of Tequila; it's traditional to drink it with salt and lime. *Patron* and *Herradura* are considered by many to be the best. (*Margaritas*, a mixed tequila drink, are popular with foreign tourists. Mexico's elite set prefers imported wine, champagne, cognac, brandy and scotch whisky.)

Mezcal, distilled from porcupine-like maguey leaves (and famous for having a *gusano* worm in each bottle, to supposedly be eaten when the bottle is empty) and *pulque*, made of maguey sap, are relatively crude brews best left for the brave.

Be aware that the high elevation of Mexico City and the rest of central Mexico will lower your tolerance to liquor. If you don't want to or can't drink, let it be known at the outset. Blaming your health or saying your doctor has ordered you not to drink are acceptable excuses.

In smaller towns, many *cantinas* (saloons, usually identifiable by their Old West-style swinging wooden doors) are still off limits to women. But in the big cities, *cantinas* have become *de moda* (fashionable) with young women, especially university students. Most Mexican men see nothing wrong with this, but some old-timers wonder what the world is coming to. Based on mysterious reasoning, some *cantinas* allow women in but prohibit them from sitting at the bar.

Being Invited to a Mexican Home

Mexicans are proud of their hospitality, as expressed by the saying *mi casa es su casa* (or *es su casa*, the short form). To be invited into a Mexican's private domain is a sign of trust that should not be taken for granted. To reject such an offer will be considered a snub. And it should be reciprocated somehow — sooner, rather than later.

If the event is scheduled for a working day, business attire is appropriate unless you are told otherwise. On a weekend, less formal but neat dress is considered appropriate. Be prepared for a late meal, probably not before 9 P.M., the earliest. It's fine to compliment the home and the way it's decorated. But don't focus on a particular item too fondly, or your host may feel obligated to give it to you.

A proper guest in Mexico waits for a signal from the host to begin eating, even if the food has been sitting on the table for some time. You should sample and praise everything served. Refusing anything offered is considered impolite, but if a certain food truly disagrees with you, say your health or your doctor forbids you to eat foods in that category. Even in the poorest homes, every effort is made to send guests home feeling uncomfortably full. Anything less than that suggests a lack of hospitality. Having plenty of leftovers is a sign of generosity — indeed, of being a good host.

If things go well, you may end up engaging in a lively discussion until late at night. There may even be dancing, or someone might pull out a guitar and begin a singalong. Still, it would be polite to offer to leave about half an hour after the meal is over. Your host will probably insist you stay longer. You will have to gauge his sincerity.

21 Socializing

The Art of Conversation

Mexicans enjoy expressing opinions and matching wits. However, cultural, political, and linguistic differences can create problems for foreigners, even in seemingly harmless small talk.

Formality. When confronted with Mexicans' extremely polite manners, non-Mexicans may feel awkward and doubt the sincerity of such ceremonial verbiage. Understand that such conventions establish mutual respect.

Openness. Despite the above, many Mexicans are quick to let down their guard and talk openly about the world and themselves. This can be intimidating for those who are not used to hearing such candor or expressing it themselves.

Wordplay. Mexicans are adept at making clever turns of phrase, and *dichos* (traditional sayings) are abundant in Mexican Spanish. Foreigners may feel lost in the midst of this kind of repartee, and developing colloquial fluency sometimes takes decades. Still, Mexicans appreciate sincere attempts by outsiders to speak their language and learn its intricacies.

Jokes. Mexicans have a great sense of humor and warmly respond to this quality in others.

Nearly every social event involves a joke-telling session. But non-Mexicans should keep in mind that humor does not usually translate well into other languages.

Be sure the joke you want to tell will work cross-culturally. If it involves a comparison between nationalities, make your own country the butt of it. This is in accordance with Mexican custom. For example, Mexicans always use the kind of joke that begins, "Presidents Clinton, Yeltsin and Zedillo are on a plane together..." to poke fun at their own president.

Touchy subjects. Given the importance Mexicans place on downplaying conflict and preserving harmony, you should avoid saying anything that might be considered offensive or insulting. People may not share your ideas about religion, and any comment an outsider makes about Mexico's political system or history can be perceived as disrespectful. If you feel compelled to say something negative about someone's country, criticize your own.

People from the United States may find themselves interrogated about U.S. policy toward immigration from Mexico, the embargo of Cuba, the country's long record of heavy-handed intervention in Latin America, or some other political issue. They should not take it personally. Remember that, historically, Mexico has been the victim of U.S. aggression and that nowhere else on earth is there such a disparity of wealth and power between two neighboring countries.

The basic rule of thumb in conversation is to steer a middle course: listen respectfully to what your counterpart has to say, agree when possible, disagree in a tactful way when appropriate.

Talking about money. Once they get to know each other, Mexicans like to talk about money: personal finances, how much things cost, and the like. Mexicans know that salaries in Mexico are typically far below those in the developed world. They may be curious to find out how much you make (or how much people in a certain occupation earn) and how much things cost in your country.

You might choose to avoid directly answering such questions by saying "not enough" or "not as much as I would like to." You might invent a low figure. If you answer honestly, be prepared to create some resentment. It may help somewhat to talk about the high cost of living in your country: the price of housing, for example, or what a beer or a kilo of tomatoes or shrimp costs.

Talking about family. Expect to be asked about your family. Mexicans often use this issue to gauge a person's values and integrity.

Socializing en La Calle

A common observation made by Mexicans who visit the United States is that the streets seem so "empty" or "lonely." Mexicans are generally more apt than their neighbors north of the border to spend time *en la calle* (literally, in the street or in public).

Traditionally, Mexicans have gravitated toward the plaza in the center of town (sometimes called *el zócalo*), particularly in the evenings and on weekends. Here, they buy snacks or crafts from street vendors, meet up with friends, have something to drink in a sidewalk cafe, or just sit on a bench and watch the world go by. In some cities, the central plaza features live orchestral music once or twice a week, and sometimes puppet shows for children. Especially in small towns, Sunday nights are reserved for strolling around the square, often to flirt with members of the opposite sex.

Crowded living conditions, especially for working-class groups, may help explain these traditions. First-time visitors to Mexico cannot help but notice the numerous pairs of *novios* (sweethearts) locked in steamy embraces in public places. (Mexicans visiting the U.S. or northern Europe are surprised to see so few couples showing affection in public.)

Films, Barbecues & Viernes Social

Some affluent Mexicans have season tickets to their city's philharmonic orchestra. But less well-to-do Mexicans also have access to the *bellas artes* (fine arts), due to subsidized ticket prices.

Mexicans throng to movie theaters and video stores. Though Hollywood dominates, Mexico has its own film industry. *Like Water for Chocolate* was a major international success.

Sunday barbecues are common. The grill is usually the man-of-the-house's domain, with the fare typically *carne asada* (grilled beef). The gender separation in such gatherings is reminiscent of suburban America in the 1950s — with the men fraternizing and drinking beer outside, while the women congregate indoors.

In fact, a good deal of Mexican socializing is a single-sex affair. Some men while away afternoons or evenings playing dominos, drinking in a *cantina*, or playing billiards in smoky parlors, where the waitress is usually the only female present. (More and more teenage girls are becoming proficient with a pool cue, however.) Women are more likely to get together at home or at a cafe.

Viernes social (Friday-night socializing) is a veritable institution in Mexico. Friends let off steam and relax in bars, restaurants, nightclubs or elsewhere. Those who can't afford to go out gather with friends at someone's house. Discotheques, "video bars," trendy cafes, and shopping malls are typical social venues for affluent Mexican youth.

Sports

Mexicans grow up playing *futból* (soccer) whenever they can. During the World Cup and other big games, the country virtually stops functioning as people glue themselves to TV sets, radios, and big screens set up in public plazas.

The exercise habit has caught on in Mexico. Many cities have jogging paths in city-run parks. Some have special bike paths. Private gyms, complete with aerobic classes, proliferate in middle class neighborhoods. Some upper-crust Mexicans play racquet sports or golf and hobnob at exclusive *clubes deportivos* (sports clubs).

Love Hotels

Moteles de paso, found on the outskirts of every Mexican city, are the setting for another form of exercise. You can call and reserve a room for the night (or more typically, *de paso*, meaning for a short time) in advance. You drive into a garage next to your room and enter the room through an interior door. Room service is delivered and bills are paid through a contraption built into the wall. Everything is designed to ensure that guests will not be seen, even by the hotels' employees.

Basic Spanish Phrases

English	Spanish
Yes	*Sí*
No	*No*
Good morning	*Buenos días*
Good afternoon	*Buenas tardes*
Good evening	*Buenas noches*
Hello	*Hola*
Good-bye	*Adiós or Que le vaya bien*
Please	*Por favor*
Thank you	*Gracias*
Pleased to meet you	*Mucho gusto*
Excuse me; I'm sorry	*Perdón*
How do you say...?	*Cómo se dice...?*
I don't understand	*No entiendo*
Do you speak English?	*Habla usted inglés?*
How much does it cost?	*Cuánto cuesta?*

23 Correspondence

Mailing Addresses

The order of information in a Mexican mailing address is basically the same as in the U.S. However, the street name comes before the number, and there is usually an extra line for the *colonia*, or district. For example:

Ing. Victor Jaime Castro Mata
Productos Químicos, S.A.
Patria 2825
Col. Degollado
Guadalajara, Jal.
44444 MEXICO

Ing. stands for *ingeniero* (engineer). *S.A.* is an abbreviation of *Sociedad Anónima*, a corporation. *Col. Degallado* is the district within Guadalajara. *Jal.* refers to the state name, Jalisco. "44444" is the postal code.

If you don't know the person's title, use *Sr.* (for *Señor*). To avoid mistaking a woman's marital status, just use her full name. It's acceptable to address mail by abbreviating the second surname as follows: *Ing. Victor Jaime Castro M.*

24   Useful Numbers

Calls within Mexico To call Mexico City, Guadalajara and Monterrey from within Mexico dial 01 + two digit city code (Mexico City 55, Guadalajara 33, Monterrey 81) + the 8 digits of the phone number. For calls to any other city in Mexico dial 01 + 3 digit city code + 7 digits of the phone number.

Calls to cell phones To call a cell phone in Mexico City, Guadalajara and Monterrey from anywhere in Mexico dial 044 + two digit long distance code (Mexico City 55, Guadalajara 33, Monterrey 81) + the 8 digits of the cell phone number. To call a cell phone in any other city in Mexico dial 044 + 3 digit long distance code + 7 digits of the cell phone number. For long distance calls to cell phones dial 01 + 2 or 3 digits (new code) + cell phone number.

International calls To call Mexico from abroad dial the access code of the country you are in + 52 + the new long distance code + 7 or 8 digit number.

City Codes

Mexico City	55
Guadalajara	33
Monterrey	81
Cancun	(998)
Chihuahua, Chihuahua	(614)

Guadalajara, Jalisco .... (33)
Juarez City, Chihuahua .... (656)
La Paz, Baja California .... (612)
Nogales, Sonora .... (631)
Puerto Vallarta, Jalisco .... (322)
San Miguel de Allende, Guanajuato .... (415)
Tijuana, Baja California .... (666)

General Information
International information 020, 090, 040
Time 030
Emergencies
(Police, Ambulance, Fire)
Emergencias 060
ABC Hospital (Mexico City)
Emergency .... (55) 5230-8161, 8162, 8163, 8164
Switchboard .... (55) 5230-8000
Red Cross Hospital (Mexico City)
Switchboard .... (55) 5580-0070
Ambulances .... (55) 5557-5757, 5395-1111
Rescue and Medical Emergencies Squad
Escuadron de Rescates y Urgencias Medicas
(ERUM) .... (55) 5722-8805
Federal Highway Police
Policia Federal de Caminos .... (55) 5677-2227
Tourist Safety
Infotur Seguridad Turística .... (55) 5250-0123
Missing Persons
Locatel .... (55) 5658-1111
Civil Protection
Protección Civil ... (55) 5683-1154, 1142, 2838, 1533
Public Safety Headquarters
Seguridad Publica Oficina Central . (55) 5242-5100
World Trade Center of Mexico City . (55) 682-9822
National Railroads of Mexico (FNM) . (55) 547-1084
Mexico City Tourist Assist. (55) 250-0123, 250-0151

25 Books & Internet Addresses

Books

Travelers' Tales: Mexico, edited by J. O'Reilly and L. Habegger. Travelers' Tales, Inc., San Francisco, California, USA, 1994. Diverse first-person accounts offer a tantalizing look at Mexican culture.

Distant Neighbors, by Alan Riding. Alfred A. Knopf, New York, USA, 1985. An insightful exploration of Mexico's history, politics, culture and the Mexican character.

Mexico Business, The Portable Encyclopedia for Doing Business with Mexico, 2nd Edition, by James L. Nolan, Ph.D. World Trade Press, Novato, California, USA, 1999. An encyclopedic view of doing business in and with Mexico. Part of the World Trade Press Country Business Guide Series.

Management in Two Cultures: Bridging the Gap Between U.S. and Mexican Managers, by Eva S. Kras. Intercultural Press, Inc., Chicago, Illinois, USA, 1988. A case study approach to cultural and management style differences between countries.

Interact: Guidelines for Mexicans and North Americans, by John C. Condon and George W. Renwick. Intercultural Press, Inc., Chicago, Illinois, USA, 1980. Focuses on how cultural differences affect style and mutual perception, and how they contribute to misunderstandings.

Hippocrene Language & Travel Guide to Mexico, by Ila Warner. Hippocrene, New York, USA, 1992. This cultural language guide presents real-life situations and the appropriate phrases for them.

La Capital: The Biography of Mexico City, by Jonathan Kendell. Random House, New York, USA, 1988. Uses the development of Mexico City as a window into the country in general.

The Mexicans: A Personal Portrait of a People, by Patrick Oster. Harper & Row, New York, USA, 1989. A fast-paced discussion of Mexican "types."

The Labyrinth of Solitude, by Octavio Paz. 1950. The Nobel-prize-winning poet's controversial exploration of the Mexican psychology. Still fascinating almost half a century after its original publication.

Internet Addresses

American Chamber of Commerce of Mexico
www.amcham.com.mx
Banco de Mexico (Central Bank of Mexico)
www.banixco.org.mx
Bancomext: Trade Commission of Mexico
www.mexico-trade.com
Banco Nacional de Comercio Exterior, S.N.C.
(Mexican Bank of Foreign Trade)
http://mexico.businessline.gob.mx
Index Mexico
www.trace-sc.com
Infosel/Terra Business Resource Guide to Mexico
www.infosel.com.mx
Inter-American Development Bank
Socio-political information for Latin America
www.iadb.org
Latin America on the Net
www.latinworld.com

Latin American Reference Network
http://lanic.utexas.edu/la/Mexico/
Mexican Institutions
Stock exchange, university listing, ministries
www.mexico-trade.com
Mexican Ministry of Tourism
www.mexicotravel.co.uk
Mexico Business
www.nafta.net/mexbiz/index.html
Mexico City Information and Resource guide
www.uas.mx
Mexico Culture Online
www.mexonline.com
Mexico Global
Online search directory in Spanish
www.mexicoglobal.com
Mexico's Index for Newspapers and Magazines
http://www.headlinespot.com/international/
americas/mexico.htm
Mexico NAFTA Resources
http://lanic.utexas.edu/la/Mexico/nafta/
Mexico's Web Guide (Spanish and English)
http://mexico.web.com.mx/
National Institute of Statistics, Geography, and Information
Instituto Nacional de Estadistica, Geografia, e Informatica
www.inegi.gob.mx
The Trade Zone
www.tradezone.com
The Yucatan Web
Top sites for Mexico travel
www.yucatanweb.com
U.S.-Mexico chamber of Commerce (in Mexico)
www.usmcoc.org

Randy Malat is a well-traveled freelance writer whose work has appeared in The Los Angeles Times and other publications. He currently lives in Guadalajara with his Mexican wife.